MW00606609

A Journey Paved in Words

Copyright © 2018 by Michael J. Forbes

All rights reserved.
No part of this publication may be reproduced in
any written, recording, electronic, or photocopying
without prior written consent of the publisher or
author.

ISBN-13: 978-0-692-19483-6
ISBN-10: 0-692-19483-5

Printed in the United States of America

Cover photo taken by: Kyle Greene-Pendelton

A Journey Paved in Words

Michael J. Forbes

Note: I am a work in progress

Contents

Selfish 1

Move 3

Let Go 4

Discomfort 5

Bend 6

Light 7

Disassociated 8

Mystery 9

Habits 10

Disconnected 11

Open Wounds 12

Healing 13

Unchained 14

Free 15

Flow 16

Release 17

Be 19

Rejection 20

Validation 21

Defiant 22

Intentional 23

Confusion 24

Stillness 25

Authenticity 26

Belonging 27

Essence 28

Distance 29

Surrender 30

Release 31

Companionship 33

Progression 34

Stripped 35

Cycle 36

Focus 37

Challenges 38

Resurface 39

Planted 40

Celebrate 41

Breathe 42

Restore 43

Pieces 44

Situations 45

Joy 46

Lessons 47

Distractions 48

Change 49

Conflict 50

Release 51

Energy 53

Character 54

Love 55

Honesty 56

Vulnerability 57

Identity 58

Walls 59

Timing 60

Rebirth 61

Closure 62

Acknowledgements 63

About the Author 64

Introduction

I sit here writing this for you who is reading this at this moment to find relevance, understanding, and community in this book. I hope that with the touch and turn of every single page, the expressed words allow you to see yourself, feel yourself, acknowledge yourself, honor yourself, appreciate yourself, and love yourself. I hope that every individual chapter allows you to take a moment to look at your own journey. I hope you're able to reflect on people, places, and things. I hope you're able to look at situations, circumstances, memories, and experiences, the good, the bad, the ugly, the all in between. I hope that when you put this book down, you are able to walk away speaking words of power over yourself.

I sit here writing this as my mother's words replay in my head per our last telephone conversation. She praised me and told me that this was it. She talked about how my words will connect with people, and that God gave me the gift to write. I sit here writing this as my father's words replay in my head as we conversed face-to-face. He told me all he wanted was for me to be happy.

I sit here writing this comforted by my parents' unconditional love, undeniable support, endless encouragement, and boundless prayers.

Selfish

It's so much easier to sit back and observe other people's situations and circumstances, listen attentively to them, and in return, give sound advice on what they should do to better their current situation and or circumstances. I can sit back and give advice all day long but when it's time to hold the mirror up to myself, self-reflect, re-evaluate, and reassess situations and circumstances of my own, that's when it really gets real. I assume turning the mirror on ourselves only forces us to look deeper within and dig into the depths of our soul as to who we are and where we currently are in that present time, place, and moment.

Many times, we are so used to giving so freely of ourselves to others we do not realize that we are leaving next to nothing for ourselves.
Those with giving and open hearts like myself, hardly notice until it's too late. By this time, your cup is just about empty, your mental state is foggy, your emotional state is unstable, your physical state is shaky, and your spiritual state is depleted. We give, we give, we give, we give, and we give some more; all the while we are being emptied on many levels within. I personally didn't realize the importance of reserving a little of myself for myself, and that it is perfectly okay at times to be selfish for my own sense of self without losing concern for other people's wellbeing.

Oftentimes, people will get comfortable with the idea that they know you will be there to meet every aching need, or be their emotional crutch of support and balance. You will have some people who will tend to constantly rely on what you give, and take as much and often as they can without any thought of reciprocating anything back in return. Again, it is perfectly okay to be there and give but be mindful of not allowing your well to run dry. I admit, there have been times I became comfortable with others giving me that crutch of comfort and support, where I probably did not realize how much they were giving while I was in the midst of whatever I was dealing with. Whether it was me needing that from others, or others realizing and taking notice that I needed such, and in return they gave. We are allowed to do this, we just have to know when to reserve a little to care for self, be there for self, and help self. So give but never forget to give to yourself what you freely give to others.

Move

When I look back over my journey and life
up to this point and the roadblocks I faced,
the times I felt hopeless like I wasn't getting
anywhere, along with the moments I felt stuck,
I never thought to go within and look at who I am.

I always thought it was others around me
be it those I knew personally near and far,
society in whole, or the world around me
that was blocking my progression and elevation.
It was only when I began to see myself go in a cycle
of what seemed to be mental and emotional
destruction, as though I was self-sabotaging myself
over and over again, that self-reflection became a
necessity.

To cope through this rollercoaster ride of emotions,
I would always go outward to deal and cope
which only allowed a temporary bandage
over the turmoil occurring inside.

All along, I was standing in the way of myself,
no one else, but me and only me.
It's easier to assume other people are
standing in the way of our personal
progression and elevation when in actuality,
it is us blocking ourselves from moving
in the direction that's best for us at that moment.
Sometimes you must get out of your own way,
but first you must confront and
work through what's going on inside.

Let Go

Letting go is an ongoing process and
should be incorporated as a daily routine.
We tend to hold on to things for far too
long that are no longer beneficial to our
being, or to who or where we are at that given
moment.

If it is no longer serving me, empowering me,
motivating me, encouraging me, inspiring me,
uplifting me, pushing me, feeding or fueling me,
then it has to go. As the adage goes,
"let go, or continue to get dragged." Let him go,
let her go, let them go, let it go.

You must get to a place to know when it's finally
time to let go. Simply let it all go or continue to be
dragged.

Discomfort

The truth will not always feel good;
many times it will make you cringe,
make you feel uneasy, place you on edge,
make you angry, and downright
uncomfortable.

That's what the truth does;
it will shake and rattle you, even bend
you only to eventually mend you.
There's growth in that discomfort,
wisdom on the other side of that uneasiness,
learning in the midst of the process,
and comfort in the ending. Whether you speak it,
hear it, see it, or live it, there will be discomfort for
comfort.

Be it you or someone else on the receiving end of it,
comfort eventually will come at the end.
I had to remind myself that truth will not always
be comfortable no matter if it's my
own or someone else's, but I do know
that comfort in the end is worth
the transitional discomfort.

Bend

Every day will not be a good day,
a great day, a joyous day, a happy day, or a fulfilled
day.

Life as we know it is an ongoing journey
that throws unforeseen curveballs on a daily basis.
Things change by the second, minute,
and hour whether we expect them to or not.

I look back over the cards dealt to me
throughout my life, and I realize
that I've been bent out of shape in more ways
than one but I didn't break,
though I was on edge many times.

Situations and circumstances whether I brought
them on myself or not, bent me so out of shape
that they couldn't help but to reshape me.
Know that it's perfectly okay to bend, but don't
break.

Light

I think about all the times I dimmed my light,
shrunk and dumbed myself down,
and held back on my greatness and magic
out of fear of other people's opinions.

If you let people hold you back, they will do just
that however, you have control over allowing that to
happen.

Rid yourself of giving excessive thought to the
opinions of others; rid yourself of fear, doubt,
hesitation, and uncertainty.

Force people to adjust to your light,
however you exude it always remain shining bright.

Disassociated

Everything and everyone are not worth my energy as this is something I have to remind myself of daily.

What we give our attention to is what our energy is attached to, and many people, places, and things are not worth it.

I remember always being told to "pick your battles wisely" and I remind myself that some battles are just not worth the energy to fight.

Be mindful of what you allow to consume your energy, everything and everyone are not worth it.

Once you empty yourself unto others, what's left for you?

Time and energy are precious, and once wasted we can't get any of it back.

Mystery

I'm open yet very private at the same time.
I find transparency and vulnerability to be
lifesaving, whether it's saving someone else's life
or my own.

You must understand that everyone doesn't deserve
the right to know every intricate and delicate part of
you.

All the in's and out's, all the good and bad,
all the joy and pain, all the happy
and sad, everyone isn't worthy of knowing every
part or piece of you.

It's a privilege to deem someone worthy enough
to allow yourself to open up and expose who you
are, and be able to share with them all your magic
and all your madness.

Habits

As we grow and evolve we break away from the old
to embrace the new.

I look back at the things I used to entertain,
the places I used to frequent, and the people I used
to surround myself with and I realize they are no
longer of interest to me.

Evolving, elevating, maturing, and journeying
through life is a process and the only thing that
remains constant is change.

You'll outgrow many people, places, and things at
different stages and phases along the way.

Don't fight it, but rather flow with it and grow with
it.

Disconnected

It's imperative to find your happy place
and break away from everything from time-to-time
and go there.

Whatever or wherever that 'happy place' is, go!
Being consumed and wrapped up in the hustle
and bustle of the realities of life can be
overwhelming at times.

Whether it's family, friends, jobs, careers,
or the basic existence of humanity around us as
we see it and live it, is more than enough at times
on its own for us to manage.

Be a little selfish with yourself every now and
then and learn to take a step back away from it all.

Open Wounds

When something easily triggers you
in a way that impacts your mood, emotions,
and state of mind, that means that wound has not
healed.

There have been many times I would allow
something said or done to me to easily disturb my
spirit.

I concluded that we all have wounds that are still
open and not yet healed, and therefore easily
pricked causing pain to resurface.

Healing

Healing is an ongoing process
that moves at its own pace therefore, it can't be
rushed.

Yet, many of us make the mistake of rushing
through healing instead of allowing the process
to move and work through us at its own time.

No matter how uncomfortable it is
and no matter how it may make us feel,
we have to realize that true healing
can't be rushed if we want it to be complete and
whole.

Unchained

How many times do you find yourself chained,
bound, and tied to the opinions of others?

Far too often, we trap and imprison ourselves
due to the fear of other people's opinions and
perceptions.

We tend to create walls around our greatness, our
power, and our entire being that diminish our full
potential, constantly extinguishing
the fire that burns deep inside of who we are.

Unchain yourself and break free from
being bound to the opinions of others.

Free

I knew there was more to life and more that
I deserved, but my vision was blurry.

That realization didn't come easy.

It came after I got sick and tired of being sick and
tired.

Have you ever sat back and looked over your life
and knew deep down that there was more for you?

Introspection brings clarity, clarity brings
realization, realization brings a new way of life,
a new way of life brings self-liberation, and
self-liberation means you're finally free.

Flow

Why force it when you can just go with the flow?

Always remember that timing is everything, and
many times we make things much harder and
complicated for ourselves than they need to be.

Don't rush it, force it, or settle for it;
it being anything or anyone that is less than what
you're worthy and deserving of.

Everything is in alignment with timing therefore,
we have to recognize and understand that timing is
in everything.

So go with the flow.

Release

Use this free space to allow yourself to feel,
express, note, affirm, create, exhale …

Release

Use this free space to allow yourself to feel,
express, note, affirm, create, exhale …

Be

Rid the idea that you must be somebody
other than who you are.

I wasted seconds, minutes, hours, days, weeks,
months, and years surrendering myself to others'
ideas of who they thought I should be.

That is time I can never reclaim, and one of the
most precious things afforded to us in life is our
time.

Stop surrendering yourself to other people
by hiding behind a guise of a false reality you
created to protect yourself.

When we do this, we are only hurting and
doing a disservice to ourselves.

Rejection

A door closing on you doesn't mean that another door won't open.

Things come, and things go, some greater than others, some smaller than others, but they will eventually come back to you.

There will be times when people will walk away from you and turn their backs on you.

Other times, there will be opportunities you were once presented that will no longer be available to you.

Whatever the situation may be, and whatever type of rejection you're up against, remind yourself that it's not the end, but rather an intermission to something greater.

Validation

It should never be about those on the outside
looking in.

Far too often we seek outside validation from
others when those on the outside can really care
less about what's going on with us on the inside.

Let go of believing and feeling things must be done
for the appeasement of others; it's not about them.

Defiant

I wasn't one to always easily challenge another
when it came to my feelings, thoughts, wants,
needs, or desires.

As I journeyed through life, lived a bit, went
through and overcame various experiences and
situations that rocked my foundation, it became
apparent that standing up and standing out was not
negotiable.

There will be times in your life and moments
that you come across where you will need
to be firm in what's for you, what's of you,
and what's not in alignment to you and who you
are.

Intentional

Showing up and being clear
with your intentions is
the key to aligning people, places,
and things accordingly
with yourself. Being clear and
intentional about our desires,
wants, and needs can eliminate
a lot of unnecessary drama,
hurt, confusion, and pain.
First, we must rid ourselves
of the fear of the unknown
based on our intentions, and
that begins with honesty.

Confusion

Over time, I find myself becoming
and unbecoming who I thought I was,
who I think I am, and who I am to be.
Confusion lies in me searching and
finding myself over-and-over again,
only to realize that I will never truly
know who I am to be as I am always
deconstructing, restructuring, reshaping,
and molding into a newer version of me.
Find comfort in knowing that there will
be many different versions of yourself as you
move through life's different phases.

Stillness

We tend to get wrapped up in always being on the go.

This place, that place, over here, over there, everywhere but where we need to be.

I'm reminding myself that life isn't a race and it doesn't need to be lived at a fast pace, and every now and then we need to practice stillness.

Authenticity

Owning and walking in your truth is
a form of power.

Showing up as our authentic-self is a daily
practice, a daily act of courage, and an indication
that we are free to simply be.

I didn't know what I was missing
until I decided to let go of who I thought
others wanted me to be, and aligned myself
with who I knew myself to always be.

Belonging

When your seat at
the table no longer
holds a place of want,
need, value, love,
acceptance, respect and
desire, then it's
time to take
your seat and occupy a
space elsewhere – at your own table.

Essence

At some point you
must realize that
someone else's perception
of you does
not have to determine
who you exist to be.
The perception of who
we are differs
from person to person.
People will perceive us
to be who they believe
us to be in different
variations and forms.
Through these varying
perceptions, we have to
remind ourselves that
we don't have to drift
away from being in tune
with who we know ourselves to truly be.

Distance

Be it near or far,
you will have to travel
the distance to see the
bigger picture of things.
Traveling doesn't
necessarily mean literally
traveling, but more so
traveling the distance
within yourself to do
some soul searching to
know what it is you
really want, who it is you
really are, what it is you
really need, and where it is
you really want to go.

Surrender

Stop forcing what
no longer is of you, and surrender
to what is for you, whatever
lies on the other side.
Despite the uncertainty,
it's certain that when
you learn to allow
things to be, they tend to
align according to
how they should be.

Release

Use this free space to allow yourself to feel,
express, note, affirm, create, exhale …

Release

Use this free space to allow yourself to feel,
express, note, affirm, create, exhale …

Companionship

We all long for it, we all
are deserving of it;
however, it's important that
we don't settle for it.

Too many people walk around filling
voids in their life with any
and everyone only to have temporary
gratification to a limited form of happiness.

We owe it to ourselves to want more than
a temporary quick fix.

Progression

No matter the pace, speed,
or distance, keep going – daily.
Just remember to keep one
foot ahead of the other, no matter
how long it takes, keep going.

Stripped

I had to unlearn everything
I was initially taught, in
order for my mind and
spirit to be stripped free
from everything I was
taught to believe. I then had
to learn on my own terms
everything I was, everything
I was not, and everything I was
eventually to be.

Cycle

Actions, patterns, circumstances,
and situations will play out
over and over again until
one says, "enough
is enough" and shifts perspective
and comes into alignment.

Focus

You will have to realign and distance
yourself from people, places,
and things that deter you from the objectives
that you have your mind set to do.

Not everyone will understand, but constantly
remind yourself – it's not for them to understand.

Challenges

Anything worthwhile won't come easy.
So prepare yourself, brace yourself,
steady yourself, and ready yourself.
The ride was never meant to
be a smooth one; we always fool ourselves
when we think otherwise.

Resurface

Whatever wants,
desires, feelings and
emotions buried deep
within, suppressed
and repressed, will
eventually come to light.
The heart always knows
what the soul
wants, even though the
mind thinks it
knows what is best for us.
Always allow the heart
to lead in order to allow
what lies deep within
to resurface.

Planted

I think about how plants are deeply
rooted in soil. I think about how
once watered, the soil moistens,
the roots expand, the leaves stretch,
rise, and become fuller and then growth is
witnessed – I see myself.
Planted, rooted, stretched, and growing.

See yourself rooted, grounded, expanding,
stretching, reshaping and growing. Sometimes
little to no water will cause our soil to dry and our
leaves to shrivel and become brittle; yet
with a little bit of water, we get a new sense
 and outlook on life – grow through what
you go through.

Celebrate

You cannot always depend
on others to acknowledge
you or see you.
When the applause stops,
when the cheers
are not there, when
the compliments fade,
then what? It is important to be
your own cheerleader – at all times.

Breathe

When it all becomes too much,
it's important to remember that
stepping away, taking some time,
inhaling and exhaling can be done
without explanation.

Restore

Take time to replenish yourself
from the inside out.
Doing too much
can lead to depletion.
Know that the mind,
just as well as the body,
fuels itself on
nourishment and care.

Pieces

Putting yourself back
together again
after shattering into
tiny parts of
who you knew
yourself to be isn't
easy.

Multiple parts
that once made
you complete, detached
and separated,
fell and scattered.

You have to know
that the intense work
you will do within
to mend the pieces of self
back together again,
will emerge a new and
improved version
of you.

Situations

Go through them,
grow through them,
explore them, study them,
embrace them,
feel them, experience them,
love them,
hate them, heal from them,
overcome them,
become anew by them, no
matter the outcome
of them.

Joy

Whatever brings you joy, do that.

Whatever brings a sense of calmness
over your spirit, indulge in that.

Whatever it is that no longer serves
a purpose to you, of you, or for you, let it go.

Do more of what makes you happy,
more of what makes you smile, more of
what makes you laugh, more of what
fulfills you, and more of what sparks the
flame your soul longs to burn for.

Lessons

I know when it's meant to be.
I know when it's not meant to be.
I know when it's real.
I know when it's not real.

To know when to let it naturally
flow, to let it be as is for the moment, for
the present time, in real time.

I remind myself that for every situation,
for every circumstance, for every
experience, there is an underlying
lesson learned that we walk away with.

Distractions

Pay attention to what easily takes
you away from what you intended to
focus on. It's easy to get sidetracked
and have your mind pulled in many
different directions if you're not careful.

Stepping away is fine; allowing yourself
to take a break is okay, shifting your energy
on something else temporarily is oftentimes
needed; but always remember why
you started.

Change

The only thing
constant is change,
whether voluntary
or involuntary.
It will not always
feel good, it will
not always be
comfortable, nor will
it always be easy;
but it is something
that will always
present itself
at some point or
another in our lives,
no matter the
timing or situation.

Conflict

Disagreement, lack of understanding,
miscommunication, and differences
are all things that challenge us as individuals.

These are things that we often can't escape or
avoid but we can change the ways
we handle and work through them.
One thing I try to work on as a daily practice
when faced with conflict from any angle is
responding instead of reacting.

Though much easier said than done, it is worth
noting that maintaining a sense of peace
over self takes priority.

Release

Use this free space to allow yourself to feel,
express, note, affirm, create, exhale ...

Release

Use this free space to allow yourself to feel,
express, note, affirm, create, exhale …

Energy

Daily interactions with
people, their physical presence,
their sound, their tone,
their vibe, their entire
being is a force
of energy, as we all are
walking and breathing sources
of energy. As someone who feels
everything so deeply,
I have to make sure
that once I'm back in my
own space, I allow
myself time to decompress
and realign.
I have to make my peace
a priority and protect
my energy – reclaim yours and make sure
it's your number one priority.

Character

They say your character
sets the tone
for your reputation.
I try to treat
people how I want to
be treated, and
how I decide to
treat them is how they
will remember me.
I think we fool ourselves
by getting so caught up
in our reputation and end
up losing sight of who
we really are. In turn,
we end up losing ourselves
to other people's views
of us. When you know who
you are, stand in it.

Love

I always thought
I could love
someone else
without wholeheartedly
loving myself,
I was wrong. The days of
pouring my blood,
sweat, and tears
into someone else
and believing that
I would get that same
or even more in
return led to disappointment
and heartache.
Heartache led to doubt,
doubt led to confusion,
confusion led to lack of
self-confidence, lack of
self-confidence led to a
lack of self-worth, and a
lack of self-worth led to
lack-of self-esteem.
You can't fully and truthfully
give to someone what
you lack and don't give
yourself because you will
always end up the one
worse off in the end.

Honesty

Time is of the essence and
the life we are afforded
is precious.
Time is not always on
our side, and the time we
spend not being honest
with ourselves and each
other is time we do not
get back. We all deserve
honesty, no matter what
lies on the other side of
its piercing truth.

Vulnerability

It's okay to expose yourself
though we're told otherwise.
When I speak of exposing,
I'm speaking from a place
of showing yourself without
any form of hesitation, to
reveal yourself free from
any mask, to share the
parts of yourself that
you've hidden, to shine
light on the areas of who
you are that's been kept
in the dark, tucked away.
It's okay to be seen for
who you are, it's okay to
be heard; we're allowed
to strip ourselves bare
at any given time when we
feel the need to and
when we choose to.

Identity

When you know who
you are, it's almost
amusing when someone
else tries to tell you
about yourself.

Make a note to self:
that is not your problem to take on.

Walls

I thought it was the other person, when it really was
me enclosed by the walls I had created for myself to
protect myself.

Shielding, guarding, restricting, not allowing the
opportunity for someone else to come in. Past
trauma did that to me; it allowed me to become a
prisoner of my own conditions, locked in by walls
of the past.

Slowly but surely, these walls I had become
accustomed to began to fall and crumble, and the
imprisoned parts of myself began to emerge as I
began to heal.

Don't rush your process and don't be quick to
demolish the walls you have become used to hiding
behind. Healing allows them to crumble at the right
time. So, be patient with yourself.

Timing

One of the hardest lessons I had to learn is that things happen accordingly on its own time. No matter what we've planned, no matter what we've envisioned, things align accordingly with its own timing.

We tend to get so caught up with other people's expectations and their timetable of how events should play out for us in our lives, not realizing that life isn't a race or competition. I had to drop the notion of wanting things to happen at a set time in my life and allow things to work freely as they should, when they should.

Rebirth

After the fire stops, the ashes settle, and the dust clears, this is when you brush yourself off and come out of what you thought would be the end of you as a new and improved version.

What I thought would be my demise, turned out to be my second coming of life.

Take what you thought would break you and use it to remake you and reshape you. There's a new life on the other side.

Closure

Old endings create room for new beginnings.
Once I allowed myself to leave a door permanently
closed, I was then able to lock it and officially turn
in my key.

I chose to no longer live where I was no longer
vested. I had to get to get a place of understanding
that closure is something that is complete, done,
over and finished.

I no longer live there anymore; I'm taking up new
residency, free from what once weighed me down
mentally, spiritually, physically, and emotionally.

Acknowledgements

I thank The Most High for granting me the gift of truth, reason, and purpose to allow my words to flow from my heart to paper.

Endless love, thanks, and gratitude to my family and friends near and far for supporting me in more ways than one. I am forever grateful and thankful for all of you.

Thank you, to my editor Morshe Araujo for rendering editing services and direction of support and feedback.

Thank you, readers and every single one of who you who purchased and read this book. I genuinely thank you from the depths of my heart. Thank you for your support and allowing a little piece of me to connect with you each time you hold this collection of truths in your hands. Even if I only reach one of you with this book, with my words, and with my experiences pulled from parts of my journey and it resonates with you, then I know that my job has been done.

Even if it's just one of you, that means you are one more soul I touched along the way.

I hope it serves you well in many ways!

Michael J. Forbes is a writer and creative from Connecticut. While straddling between intersections of communities, he shines light on the realities of life from a lens of his own on race, culture, identity, and his day-to-day existence of life through his words and personal lived experiences.

www.MichaelJForbes.com

Made in the USA
Middletown, DE
10 February 2023

23640712R00043